The Power of Gratitude

365 Quotes and Scriptures for Healing
Your Mind, Body, and Heart

C. Chérie Hardy

Avant-garde Books

Avant-garde Books
Spiritual Division
Post Office Box 566
Mableton, Georgia 30126
www.avantgardebooks.net

The Power of Gratitude
365 Quotes and Scriptures for Healing Your Mind, Body and
Heart
Copyright © 2013 by C. Chérie Hardy
All rights reserved.

ISBN: 978-0-9743676-9-9

This book is dedicated to:

Dr. Margie Jenkins

Margie,
This book is a direct result of my gratitude for all the
beautiful people that God has placed in my life. I want
you to know that I am appreciative of the wise counsel
you inculcated in me during a challenging season of my
career. Thank you for encouraging me to stay strong
and positive. I am immensely grateful that you refused to
let me complain and waddle in my frustration and grief.
May God bless you with a thousand times more than
you gave to me!

"The LORD is gracious and full of compassion, slow to anger and great in mercy. The LORD is good to all, and His tender mercies are over all His works."
–Psalm 145:8-9 (NKJV)

Dear Reader:

The Power of Gratitude: 365 Quotes and Scriptures for Healing Your Mind, Body and Heart is a God-inspired book that provides timeless wisdom and encouragement relating to one of life's most important and transformative ingredients, GRATITUDE.

Having a grateful heart is like taking an effective, restorative medicine which is absolutely free, and has no adverse side effects. Being thankful, in spite of uncomfortable circumstances, allows us to *see* that there is so much beauty around us. As we focus on what we have, instead of what we don't, we can get greater clarity about the root of our turmoil which transforms our perception of difficult situations. With "grateful eyes" we can see the priceless treasures in our tribulation; as well as the light shining through life's dark clouds.

Countless times throughout my life I have witnessed and experienced the power of gratitude which so often became the genesis of physical healing as well as spiritual awakening. I've learned that while it takes mental fortitude and spiritual discipline, we have the ability to shift our focus from our struggles and meditate on the positive aspects of our lives—the things that aren't broken and battered. When we are thankful and concentrate on the good emanating within us and around us, we are able to experience a preternatural contentment and peace.

Thus, gratitude becomes the spiritual conduit through which we discover the grace of God, especially during stressful seasons of our lives. Moreover, an attitude of gratitude helps us realize that our loving Heavenly Fathers will sometimes let the rain fall so that His flowers can grow. By fully embracing God's unfailing love, we can smile in the midst of hardship knowing that He is faithful to bring nourishing sunshine after every storm. He is bigger than our problems and more powerful than our pain. We simply must accept that no matter what we're facing, there is always something to celebrate and for which to be GRATEFUL.

It is my greatest hope that this book reminds you of gratitude's power to heal your mind, body, and heart. Remember, "Be anxious for nothing, but in everything by prayer and supplication with thanksgiving, let your requests be known to God; and the peace of God, which surpasses all understanding, will guard your hearts and minds through Jesus Christ."
-Philippians 4: 6-7 (NKJV)

With love,
C. Chérie Hardy

The Power

of

Gratitude

365 Quotes and Scriptures for Healing
Your Mind, Body, and Heart

C. Chérie Hardy

January 1

"God gave you a gift of 86,400 seconds today. Have you used one to say, 'thank you'?" –William Arthur Ward

January 2

"To be grateful is to recognize the Love of God in everything He has given us—and He has given us everything. Every breath we draw is a gift of His love; every moment of existence is a grace, for it brings with it the immense graces from Him. Gratitude therefore takes nothing for granted; is never unresponsive; and is constantly awakening to new wonder and to praise of the goodness of God. " –Thomas Merton

1

"The person who hasn't ever endured difficult circumstances hasn't been born. Trouble is inevitable for all of us; there is nothing we can do to avoid it. When we nurture a grateful heart, and decide to focus on what is right in our lives rather than what we *perceive* is wrong; we discover rich spiritual treasures buried deep beneath our tribulation. It starts with focusing on what we have instead of what we don't; and searching for the good in what we *think* is bad. Gratitude makes us smile in spite of our problems. Its transformative power helps us see light in the midst of darkness. It allows us to make sense of what seems incomprehensible on the surface."

–C. Chérie Hardy

January 4

"You pray in your distress and in your need; would that you might pray also in the fullness of your joy and in your days of abundance." –Kahlil Gibran

January 5

"Do not spoil what you have by desiring what you have not; remember that what you now have was once among the things you only hoped for." –Epicurus

January 6

"Let us be grateful to the people who make us happy; they are the charming gardeners who make our souls blossom."
–Marcel Proust

January 7

"When it comes to life the critical thing is whether you take things for granted or take them with gratitude." –G. K. Chesterton

January 8

"Finally, brethren, whatever things are true, whatever things are noble, whatever things are just, whatever things are pure, whatever things are lovely, whatever things are of good report, if there is any virtue and if there is anything praiseworthy—meditate on these things." –Philippians 4:8 (NKJV)

January 9

"Gratitude is not only the greatest of virtues, but the parent of all others."
–Marcus Tullius Cicero

January 10

"Develop an attitude of gratitude, and give thanks for everything that happens to you, knowing that every step forward is a step toward achieving something bigger and better than your current situation."
–Brian Tracy

January 11

"Gratitude bestows reverence, allowing us to encounter everyday epiphanies, those transcendent moments of awe that change forever how we experience life and the world." –John Milton

January 12

"Make a joyful shout to God, all the earth! Sing out the honor of His name; Make His praise glorious." –Psalm 66:1-2 (NKJV)

January 13

"Everything we do should be a result of our gratitude for what God has done for us." –Lauryn Hill

January 14

"It is good for me that I have been afflicted, that I may learn Your statutes. The law of Your mouth is better to me than thousands of coins of gold and silver." –Psalm 119:71-72 (NKJV)

January 15

"Feeling down? Find a quiet place and start making a list of all the good things in your life. The truth is that you don't have enough paper to record every blessing from God. The fact that you can breathe is evidence that God still has some work for you to do on Earth—and that He hasn't brought you this far to abandon you. Be grateful that He thinks so highly of you."
–C. Chérie Hardy

January 16

"I can see the glass half full and thank God for what I have." –Ann Monnar

January 17

"Of all the characteristics needed for both a happy and morally decent life, none surpasses gratitude. Grateful people are happier and grateful people are more morally decent." ~Dennis Prager

January 18

"Let the first words that come from your mouth each morning be, 'thank you for everything, Heavenly Father. I can do nothing without You. May You get glory from your servant.'"~C. Chérie Hardy

January 19

"The deepest craving of human nature is the need to be appreciated."
~William James

January 20

"I will lift up my eyes to the hills—from whence comes my help? My help comes from the LORD, who made heaven and earth. He will not allow your foot to be moved; He who keeps you will not slumber."
–Psalm 121:1-3 (NKJV)

January 21

"You simply will not be the same person two months from now after consciously giving thanks each day for the abundance that exists in your life. And you will have set in motion an ancient spiritual law: the more you have and are grateful for, the more you will be given." –Sarah Ban Breathnach

January 22

"We must decide to thank God for ALL of our experiences even those which seem uncomfortable, frightening and overwhelming. I have learned that God uses all of our pain for a purpose. He doesn't waste our suffering. There are many lessons we learn by "going through" trouble. The greatest of these is how to trust and depend on His incomprehensible love for us." ~C. Chérie Hardy

January 23

"We think we have to do something to be grateful or something has to be done in order for us to be grateful, when gratitude is a state of being." ~Iyanla Vanzant

January 24

"Act on your gratitude for someone special in your life. Whether it is in a grand or small way, *show* that person just how thankful you are to God that he or she is in your life."
~C. Chérie Hardy

January 25

"Oh give thanks to the LORD, for He is good! For His mercy endures forever."
~Psalm 136:1 (NKJV)

January 26

"When eating bamboo sprouts, remember the man who planted them."
~Chinese Proverb

January 27

"As we express our gratitude, we must never forget that the biggest appreciation is not to utter words, but to live by them."
–John F. Kennedy

January 28

"LORD, You have been our dwelling place in all generations. Before the mountains were brought forth, or ever You had formed the earth and the world, even from everlasting to everlasting, You are God." –Psalm 90:1-2 (NKJV)

January 29

"Gratitude is an opener for locked-up blessings." –Marianne Williamson

January 30

"Both abundance and lack exist simultaneously in our lives, as parallel realities. It is always our conscious choice which secret garden we will tend... when we choose not to focus on what is missing from our lives but grateful for the abundance that's present—love, health, family, friends, work, the joys of nature and personal pursuits that bring us pleasure—the wasteland of illusion falls away and we experience Heaven on earth."
~Sarah Ban Breathnach

January 31

"If you want to turn your life around, try thankfulness. It will change your life mightily." ~Gerald Good

13

February 1

"There are two kinds of gratitude: the sudden kind we feel for what we take; the larger kind we feel for what we give."
–Edwin Arlington Robinson

February 2

"Let gratitude be the pillow upon which you kneel to say your nightly prayer. And let faith be the bridge you build to overcome evil and welcome good." –Maya Angelou

February 3

"No matter what is happening inside you or around you, take a moment to stop and smile. Remember, a joyful moment. Thank God for past victories and a future that is filled with more smiles." –C. Chérie Hardy

February 4

"A person however learned and qualified in his life's work in whom gratitude is absent, is devoid of that beauty of character which makes personality fragrant."
–Hazrat Inayat Khan

February 5

"Be anxious for nothing, but in everything by prayer and supplication, with thanksgiving, let your requests be made known to God; and the peace of God, which surpasses all understanding, will guard your hearts and minds through Christ Jesus." –Philippians 4:6-7 (NKJV)

February 6
"Gratitude is a quality similar to electricity: it must be produced and discharged and used up in order to exist at all."
—William Faulkner

February 7
"...the grateful person knows that God is good, not by hearsay but by experience. And that is what makes all the difference."
–Thomas Merton

February 8
"It's a sign of mediocrity when you demonstrate gratitude with moderation."
–Roberto Benigni

February 9
"The highest tribute to the dead is not grief but gratitude." –Thornton Wilder

February 10
"When we become more fully aware that our success is due in large measure to the loyalty, helpfulness, and encouragement we have received from others, our desire grows to pass on similar gifts. Gratitude spurs us on to prove ourselves worthy of what others have done for us. The spirit of gratitude is a powerful energizer."
–Wilferd A. Peterson

February 11

"We learned about gratitude and humility—
that so many people had a hand in our
success, from the teachers who inspired us
to the janitors who kept our school clean...
and we were taught to value everyone's
contribution and treat everyone with
respect."–Michelle Obama

February 12

"What I've learned is there's a scientifically
proven phenomenon that's attached to
gratitude and that if you consciously take
note of what is good in your life,
quantifiable benefits happen."
–Deborah Neville

February 13
"Don't let a day start and end without thanking God for His unconditional, immeasurable and never-ending love for you." ~C. Chérie Hardy

February 14
"God, if I had ten trillion tongues they wouldn't be enough to thank you for your love." ~Author Unknown

February 15
"No one who achieves success does so without acknowledging the help of others. The wise and confident acknowledge this help with gratitude."
~Alfred North Whitehead

February 16
"Just an observation: it is impossible to be both grateful and depressed. Those with a grateful mindset tend to see the message in the mess and even though life may knock them down, the grateful find reasons, if even small ones, to get up." –Steve Maraboli

February 17
"Blessed are those who can give without remembering and receive without forgetting."–Author Unknown

February 18
"The struggle ends when gratitude begins." –Neale Donald Walsh

February 19

"Close your eyes. When you open them, what is the first thing you see? Thank God for your physical eyesight. Most importantly, thank Him for correcting your spiritual vision about the past and strengthening your *insight* for the future."
–C. Chérie Hardy.

February 20

"Given the amount of unjust suffering and unhappiness in the world, I am deeply grateful for, sometimes perplexed by, how much misery I have been spared."
–Dennis Prager

February 21

"Be thankful for what you have; you'll end up having more. If you concentrate on what you don't have, you will never, ever have enough." –Oprah Winfrey

February 22

"Oh give thanks to the God of gods! For His mercy endures forever."
–Psalm 136:2 (NKJV)

February 23

"There is not a more pleasant exercise of the mind than gratitude. It is accompanied with such inward satisfaction that the duty is sufficiently rewarded by the performance." –Joseph Addison

February 24

"Do not take anything for granted—not one smile or one person or one rainbow or one breath, or one cozy night in your bed."
–Terri Guillemets

February 25

"Change your expectation for appreciation and the world changes instantly."
–Tony Robbins

February 26

"When you count all your assets, you always show a profit." –Robert Quillen

February 27
"Whenever we are appreciative, we are filled with a sense of well-being and swept up by the feeling of joy." –M. J. Ryan

February 28
"Happiness cannot be traveled to, owned, earned, worn or consumed. Happiness is the spiritual experience of living every minute with love, grace and gratitude."
–Denis Waitley

February 29
"Be thankful for the people in your life who make you a priority rather than an option; those who demonstrate through their actions that they love you unconditionally."
–C. Chérie Hardy

March 1

"It is good to give thanks to the LORD, and to sing praises of Your name, O Most High; to declare Your lovingkindness in the morning and Your faithfulness every night."
–Psalm 92:1-2 (NKJV)

March 2

"Gratitude is the music of the heart, when its chords are swept by the breeze of kindness." –Author Unknown

March 3

"We must never take for granted even the tiniest gesture of kindness. We must learn how to thank God for both big and small blessings."—C. Chérie Hardy

March 4
"Gratitude changes the pangs of [bad memories] into a tranquil joy."
–Dietrich Bonhoeffer

March 5
"Courtesies of a small and trivial character are the ones which strike deepest in the grateful and appreciating heart."
–Henry Clay

March 6
"We can only be said to be alive in those moments when our hearts are conscious of our treasures." –Thornton Wilder

March 7

"Even though my life hasn't been a 'crystal stair', when I think about how many steps God has helped me climb, I want to run and shout with joy."
~C. Chérie Hardy

March 8

"The LORD is my strength and my shield; my heart trusted in Him, and I am helped; therefore, my heart greatly rejoices; and with my song I will praise Him."
~Psalm 28:7 (NKJV)

March 9

"Gratitude isn't a burdening emotion."
~Loretta Young

March 10

"Gratitude is an effective, yet inexpensive medicine that can cure sorrow and depression. Have you had a dose of it, today?" –C. Chérie Hardy

March 11

"Gratitude helps you grow and expand; gratitude brings joy and laughter into your life and into the lives of all those around you." –Eileen Caddy

March 12

"I will praise the name of God with a song, and will magnify Him with thanksgiving." –Psalm 69:30 (NKJV)

March 13

"Reflect upon your present blessings, of which every man has plenty; not on your past misfortunes of which all men have some." ~Charles Dickens

March 14

"Gratitude is the ability to experience life as a gift. It liberates us from the prison of self-preoccupation." ~John Ortberg

March 15

"Hem your blessings with thankfulness so they don't unravel." ~Author Unknown

March 16

"Gratitude opens the door to...the power, the creativity of the universe. You open the door through gratitude." –Deepak Chopra

March 17

"I will give to the Lord the thanks due to his righteousness, and I will sing praise to the name of the Lord, the Most High."
–Psalm 7:17 (ESV)

March 18

"As I look back with gratitude for the loved ones and opportunities that have brought me great joy and fulfillment, I also enjoy the fullness of this present moment. Right now, I am making memories for the years to come."
–Daily Word, 2013

March 19

"God doesn't love us less because He doesn't immediately rescue us from difficult circumstances. There is a reason why He allows us to face hardship. When we are grateful, we will discover that we always gain spiritual blessings and so much more through our pain." ~C. Chérie Hardy

March 20

"To speak gratitude is courteous and pleasant, to enact gratitude is generous and noble, but to live gratitude is to touch Heaven."—Johannes A. Gaertner

March 21
"Saying thank you is more than good manners. It is good spirituality."
–Alfred Painter

March 22
"What you truly acknowledge truly is yours. Invite your heart to be grateful and your thank-you's will be heard even when you don't use words." –Pavithra Mehta

March 23
"The roots of all goodness lie in the soil of appreciation for goodness."
—Tenzin Gyatso

March 24

"Thank God for your parents regardless of the character they modeled for you as a child. God chose the parents He wanted you to have. If they were nurturing and kind, they have given you a great example to follow; if they were abusive and neglectful, they have shown you what not to do. God not only wants you to continue building legacies of noble character, He also wants you to break negative cycles in your family. Thank Him for the opportunity to do this."
~C. Chérie Hardy

March 25

"Gratitude for the seemingly insignificant—a seed—this [is what] plants the giant miracle." ~Ann Voskamp

March 26

"If we had no winter, the spring would not be so pleasant; if we did not sometimes taste adversity, prosperity would not be so welcome." ~Anne Bradstreet

March 27

"Make the Creator smile by telling Him, 'thank you'."—C. Chérie Hardy

March 28

"Through the LORD's mercies we are not consumed, because His compassions fail not. They are new every morning; great is [His] faithfulness."
~Lamentations 3:22-23 (NKJV)

March 29

"I would rather be able to appreciate things I cannot have rather than have things I am not able to appreciate."—Elbert Hubbard

March 30

"We tend to forget that happiness doesn't come as a result of getting something we don't have, but rather recognizing and appreciating what we do have."
–Fredrick Koeing

March 31

"At times our own light goes out and is rekindled by a spark from another person. Each of us has cause to think with deep gratitude of those who have lighted the flame within us. "–Albert Schweitzer

April 1
"If you can't reward, then you should thank."
~Arabic Proverb

April 2
"Stop thinking that gratitude is a by-product of your circumstances and start thinking of it as a world view."
~Bryan Robles

April 3
"Real life isn't always going to be perfect or go our way, but the recurring acknowledgement of what is working in our lives can help us not only to survive but surmount our difficulties."
~Sarah Ban Breathnach

April 4
"Once we discover how to appreciate timeless values in our daily experiences, we can enjoy the best things in life."
~Harry Hepner

April 5
"Be very grateful if you can read. Now activate your gratitude by teaching others."
~C. Chérie Hardy

April 6
"This might seem like a radical thought, but be grateful when someone maliciously hurts you. Use your experience as a powerful lesson for what NOT to do to others."
~C. Chérie Hardy

April 7

"I still miss those I loved who are no longer with me but I find I am grateful for having loved them. The gratitude has finally conquered the loss." –Rita Mae Brown

April 8

[Gratitude during unpleasant times] is like a butterfly which, when pursued, is always beyond our grasp, but if you will sit quietly, may alight upon you."
–Nathaniel Hawthorne

April 9

"There is no such thing as gratitude unexpressed. If it is unexpressed, it is plain, old-fashioned ingratitude." –Robert Brault

April 10
"There are only two things that can
destroy memories: death and disease.
When we are grateful, we will learn to thank
God for not erasing the bad ones, but
healing them so that they become
empowering instead of crippling."
–C. Chérie Hardy

April 11
"Among the things you can give and still
keep are your word, a smile and a grateful
heart." –Zig Ziglar

April 12
"Acknowledging the good that you already
have in your life is the foundation for all
abundance." –Eckhart Tolle

April 13

"Oh, give thanks to the LORD! Call upon His name; make known His deeds among the peoples! Sing to Him, sing psalms to Him; talk of all His wondrous works!"
– 1 Chronicle 16:8-9 (NKJV)

April 14

"Gratitude is riches. Complaint is poverty."
–Doris Day

April 15

"We would worry less if we praised [God] more. Thanksgiving is the enemy of discontent and dissatisfaction."
–Harry Ironside

April 16

"Gratitude isn't a tool to manipulate the universe or God. It's a way to acknowledge our faith that everything happens for a reason even if we don't know what that reason is." ~Melody Beattie

April 17

"Do what you can with what you have, where you are." ~Theodore Roosevelt

April 18

"Gratitude makes you look better while resentment, unforgiveness, and anger make you look bitter." ~C. Chérie Hardy

April 19
"What if you gave someone a gift, and [he or she] neglected to say thank you—would you be likely to give another? Life is the same way. In order to attract more of the blessings that life has to offer, you must truly appreciate what you already have."
–Ralph Marston

April 20
"When a person doesn't have gratitude, something is missing in his or her humanity."
–Elie Wiesel

April 21
"It's a poor frog who doesn't praise its own pond." –Author Unknown

April 22

"My riches consist not in the extent of my possessions, but in the fewness of my wants." ~Joseph Brotherton

April 23

"A miracle happens when you repeatedly say the words, 'thank you, Lord,' aloud. You inexplicably start to feel better." ~C. Chérie Hardy

April 24

"The miracle of gratitude is that it shifts your perception to such an extent that it changes the world you see." ~Robert Holden

April 25
"Gratitude is the first sign of a thinking, rational creature." –Solanus Casey

April 26
"A man was ungrateful that all he had to eat was a banana until he saw someone eat the banana peel that he had just thrown over the hill." –George E. McRae

April 27
"Remember the things in life that are free to each of us—our family, our friends, our soul, our hopes, our dreams, and our knowledge—are the most important." –Jaren L. Davis

April 28

"If you want to confuse the devil, start to praise and worship God in the midst of heartache." –David S. Beacham, Jr.

April 29

"You lose nothing when you express gratitude for what is good in your life, but you gain sorrow when your focus on your problems." –C. Chérie Hardy

April 30

"That action is not warrantable which either fears to ask the divine blessing on its performance, or having succeeded, does not come with thanksgiving to God for its success." –Francis Quarles

May 1
"One minute of sincere gratitude can wash away a lifetime's disappointments."
—Silvia Hartmann

May 2
"Find a really quiet place to reflect about the times when something *almost* happened, but it didn't for one reason or another. God's grace kept you in the past and it will continue to sustain you in the future. Unlike many men, God is consistent; He doesn't deviate from His goodness. Thank God for future blessings right now."
-C. Chérie Hardy

May 3

"There is a calmness to a life lived in gratitude, a quiet joy." –Ralph H. Blum

May 4

"The problem with a victim mentality is that we forget to see the blessings of the day. Because of this, our spirit is poisoned instead of nourished." –Steve Maraboli

May 5

"I have learned silence from the talkative, tolerance from the intolerant, and kindness from the unkind. I should not be ungrateful to these teachers." –Khalil Gibran

May 6

"Be grateful for the people who listen to you. Listening is an act of humility and love. Treasure the people who sacrifice their time to willingly listen to you, without judgment and condemnation. They are treasures worth more than gold."
–C. Chérie Hardy

May 7

"Even the smallest tender mercy can bring peace when recognized and appreciated."
–Richelle E. Goodrich

May 8

"But he who is of a merry heart has a continual feast."
–Proverbs 15:15b (NKJV)

May 9

"Find the light. Reach for it. Live for it. Pull yourself up by it. Gratitude always makes for straighter, taller trees." –Al R. Young

May 10

"When we give cheerfully and accept gratefully, everyone is blessed."
–Maya Angelou

May 11

"Be thankful for your allotment in an imperfect world. Though better circumstances can be imagined, far worse are nearer misses than you probably care to realize." –Richelle E. Goodrich

May 12
"See that no one renders evil for evil to anyone, but always pursue what is good both for yourselves, and for all. Rejoice always, pray without ceasing. In everything give thanks for this is the will of God in Christ Jesus for you."
-1 Thessalonians 5:15-18 (NKJV)

May 13
"Gratitude gives you a spiritual facelift."
-C. Chérie Hardy

May 14
"To live a life fulfilled, reflect on the things you have with gratitude." -Jaren L. Davis

May 15

"Life doesn't owe us anything. We only owe ourselves, to make the most of the life we are living, of the time we have left, and to live in gratitude." ~Bronnie Ware

May 16

"In normal life we hardly realize how much more we receive than we give, and life cannot be rich without such gratitude. It is so easy to overestimate the importance of our own achievements compared with what we owe to the help of others."
~Dietrich Bonhoeffer

May 17

"As each day comes to us refreshed and anew, so does my gratitude renew itself daily. The breaking of the sun over the horizon is my grateful heart drawing upon a blessed world." –Terri Guillemets

May 18

"Sing praise to the LORD, you saints of His, and give thanks at the remembrance of His holy name. For His anger is but for a moment, his favor is for life; weeping may endure for a night, but joy comes in the morning." –Psalm 30:4-5 (NJKV)

May 19

"Thank God for great spiritual teachers. Throughout the history of mankind, God has used men and women to articulate His will. These people were not chosen for their perfection, but because they had a relationship with Him. In spite of all the disheartening news reports about ministers falling from grace, there are some mighty men and women of valor who genuinely care about people's souls."
—C. Chérie Hardy

May 20

"This is the day that the Lord has made; let us rejoice and be glad in it."
—Psalm 118:24 (ESV)

May 21

"A sensible thanksgiving for mercies received is a mighty prayer in the Spirit of God. It prevails with Him unspeakably."
~John Bunyan

May 22

"Give unto the LORD, O you mighty ones, give unto the LORD glory and strength. Give unto the LORD the glory due to His name; worship the LORD in the beauty of holiness."
~Psalm 29:1-2 (NKJV)

May 23

"Ingratitude produces pride while gratitude produces humility." ~Orrin Woodward

May 24

"Even in the most peaceful surroundings, the angry heart finds quarrel. Even in the most quarrelsome surroundings, the grateful heart finds peace." –Doe Zantamata

May 25

"Gratitude is the sweetest thing in a seeker's life—in all human life. If there is gratitude in your heart, then there will be tremendous sweetness in your eyes."
–Sri Chinmoy

May 26

"We must find time to stop and thank the people who make a difference in our lives."
–John F. Kennedy

May 27

"True happiness is to enjoy the present, without anxious dependence upon the future, not to amuse ourselves with hopes or fears but to rest satisfied [and be grateful] with what we have, which is sufficient, for he that is so wants nothing. The greatest blessings of mankind are within us and within our reach. A wise man is content with his lot, whatever it may be, without wishing for he has not." –Lucius Annaeus Seneca

May 28

"Some people grumble that roses have thorns; I am grateful that thorns have roses."
–Alphonse Karr

May 29

"Gratitude is one of God's prescriptions for pain. Gratitude has the power to cure depression, anxiety, fear, loneliness, apathy, and so much more. It's an effective medicine for a broken heart and tortured mind. It has no adverse side effects and toxic chemicals. Moreover, it's free and has no expiration date. Gratitude changes how we see things. It heals our attitude so when can embrace the message in our mess; discover treasures in our trials; transform obstacles into opportunities; understand the countless blessings behind our burdens. Ingratitude is like a tumor that must be removed or it will grow and become malignant to us in a myriad of ways." –C. Chérie Hardy

May 30

"If the only prayer you said was 'thank you', that would be enough." –Meister Eckhart

May 31

"Be grateful that God never lets us forget that our days are numbered. Precious moments zoom past us faster than we expect. This means that we cannot afford to squander this limited time. The knowledge of our mortality can teach us how to be grateful for time we get that was never promised to us in the first place. It is imperative that our thoughts, words and deeds be an expression of gratitude for God's daily mercy and grace."
–C. Chérie Hardy

June 1

"I have learned to thank God for what I don't have in my life. If I needed something as much as I thought I did, I would have it right now." ~C. Chérie Hardy

June 2

"Gratitude is not only the memory but the homage of the heart rendered to God for his goodness." ~Nathaniel Parker Willis

June 3

"Let us rise up and be thankful, for if we didn't learn a lot today, at least we learned a little, and if we didn't learn a little, at least we didn't get sick, and if we got sick, at least we didn't die; so, let us all be thankful."
~Siddhartha Gautama

June 4
"Gratitude is the inward feeling of kindness received. Thankfulness is the natural impulse to express that feeling. Thanksgiving is the following of that impulse." ~Henry Van Dyke

June 5
"Joy is the simplest form of gratitude."
~Karl Barth

June 6
"We ought to shout out our thanksgiving as if every war were over; as if there were no big taxes; as if there were no sickness, no crime." ~John R. Rice

"I often remind myself that no matter how challenging my job becomes at times, it is better than slavery. If God places me on a job that feels like a dry desert, it might be because He wants me to be an oasis for my co-workers and the people He has ordained me to serve. God needs *His* advocates in every arena of life. We can't do His work in a place where it is not needed. Sometimes that place is where we are appreciated the least, yet we can thank God for the opportunity to be used by Him." ~C. Chérie Hardy

June 8
"Keep calm and be thankful."
~Author Unknown

June 9

"Because gratitude is the key to happiness, anything that undermines gratitude must undermine happiness. And nothing undermines gratitude as much as expectations. There is an inverse relationship between expectations and gratitude: the more expectations you have, the less gratitude you have."
~Dennis Prager

June 10

"The happy heart runs with the river, floats on the air, lifts to the music, soars with the eagle, and hopes with the prayer."
~Maya Angelou

June 11

"There are days when I wake up and thank God for not answering some of my prayers. If He had, I would have suffered greatly. I now know that His perfect wisdom will always be greater than my misguided desire." ~C. Chérie Hardy

June 12

"Let the peoples praise You, O God; let all the peoples praise You. Oh, let the nations be glad and sing for joy! For You shall judge the people righteously, and govern the nations on earth."
~Psalm 67:3-4 (NKJV)

June 13

"True gratitude can never come from the mind. It has to flow from the heart to the mind, vitals and body until everything that we have and are is a sea of gratitude."
–Sri Chinmoy

June 14

"It doesn't matter if the glass is half empty or half full... Be grateful that you have a glass, and there is something in it."
–Emily Campiere

June 15

"Do you want to learn French? Start with these two words: 'Merci beaucoup.'"
–C. Chérie Hardy

June 16

"I will bless the LORD at all times; His praise shall continually be in my mouth. My soul shall make its boast in the LORD; the humble shall hear of it and be glad. Oh, magnify the LORD with me, and let us exalt His name together."
–Psalm 34:1-3 (NKJV)

June 17

"I can never thank God enough for His forgiveness. To know that God desires to pardon my transgression fills me with humility, peace, and gratitude. Forgiveness is one of His many preternatural acts of love that I cannot fully understand and deserve." –C. Chérie Hardy

June 18
"Praise the bridge that carried you over."
~George Colman

June 19
"Offer to God a sacrifice of thanksgiving, and perform your vows to the Most High."
~Psalm 50:14 (ESV)

June 20
"Gratitude opens your eyes to limitless potential to the universe, while dissatisfaction closes your eyes to it."
~Stephens Richards

June 21

"Here are the two best prayers I know: 'help me, help me, help me' and 'thank you, thank you, thank you'". –Anne Lamott

June 22

"Grace isn't a little prayer you chant before receiving a meal. It's a way to live."
–Jacqueline Winspear

June 23

"No man has ever lived that had enough of children's gratitude or a woman's love."
–William Butler Yeats

June 24

"Let us thank God for prayer warriors—the people who petition the Most High on our behalf. Success, in any form, is a direct result of sincere prayer. Let us always be grateful for our ancestors who offered ancient prayers that went out long before we were conceived. Let us rejoice in knowing that there are people in our lives who take the time to ask God to bless and guide us. I am still here because of the loving, fervent prayers of faithful people. And, so are you. Be grateful."
–C. Chérie Hardy

June 25

"Rest and be thankful."
–William Wadsworth

June 26

"Give thanks in all circumstances; for this is the will of God in Christ Jesus for you."
–1 Thessalonians 5:18 (ESV)

June 27

"In life one has a choice to take one of two paths: to wait for some special day—or to celebrate each [day as special]."
–Rasheed Ogunlaru

June 28

"Find things to be grateful for. It is easy. You're alive; that's a good thing to start being grateful for right away."
–Allan G. Hunter

June 29

"When gratitude dominates our minds, we feel better. This allows us to be more productive and effective representatives of God." –C. Chérie Hardy

June 30

"Thanksgiving for God's faithfulness in our pain is the indisputable proof that we believe God is a part of our pain."
–Erwin W. Lutzer

July 1

"'Thank you' is a wonderful phrase. Use it. It will add stature to your soul."
–Marjorie Pay Hinckley

July 2

"Silent gratitude isn't very much to anyone."—Gertrude Stein

July 3

"Those blessings are sweetest that are won with prayer and worn with thanks."
–Thomas Goodwin

July 4

"The freedom to choose how we respond to any situation is one of the greatest gifts God has given each of us. While we cannot control everything that happens to us, we can control our attitude. Let us never fail to express our gratitude to God for giving us this awesome gift of choice."
–C. Chérie Hardy

July 5
"Don't kneel to me, that is not right. You must kneel to God only, and thank Him for the liberty you will hereafter enjoy."
–Abraham Lincoln

July 6
"God needs no worship; no praise; and no thanksgiving. It is man himself who needs the benefit to be derived from these activities."
–Paul Brunton

July 7
"We pray for big things and forget to give thanks for the ordinary, small (and yet really not small) gifts." –Dietrich Bonhoeffer

July 8

"When I am focused on unpleasant things in life, the ego is steering the ship, albeit through treacherous storms. When my awareness shifts to presence and gratitude, the Divine gently guides me through still waters." –Dean Jackson

July 9

"I called on the LORD in distress; the LORD answered me and set me in a broad place. The LORD is on my side; I will not fear. What can man do to me?"
–Psalm 118:5-6 (NKJV)

July 10

"Feeling gratitude and not expressing it is like wrapping a present and not giving it."
–William Arthur Ward

July 11

"Thankfulness is the soil in which pride does not grow easily." –Michael Ramsay

July 12

"We should certainly count our blessings, but we should also make our blessings count." –Neal A. Maxwell

July 13

"We can learn how to be generous because of selfishness; we can learn how to be grateful for patience when we survive the consequences of impatience; we can learn how to be more appreciative of love because of being hated; and we can learn how to cherish peace after enduring chaos. We just have to learn how to be grateful for *all* circumstances."

~C. Chérie Hardy

July 14

"Never let the things you want make you forget the things you have."

~Author Unknown

July 15

"One of the main reasons that we lose our enthusiasm in life is because we become ungrateful...we let what was once a miracle become common to us. We get so accustomed to his goodness it becomes routine." –Joel Osteen

July 16

"Oh give thanks to the Lord, for he is good, for his steadfast love endures forever! Let the redeemed of the Lord say so, whom he has redeemed from trouble."
–Psalm 107:1-2 (ESV)

July 17

"Count your rainbows, instead of your thunderstorms." –Author Unknown

July 18
"Be consistent in showing your gratitude to others. Gratitude is a fuel, a medicine, and spiritual and emotional nourishment."
–Steve Maraboli

July 19
"Be grateful for the people who model how to endure hard times with God's grace and dignity. They show us how to be grateful for spiritual redemption. Their strength encourages us to remain focused on God."
–C. Chérie Hardy

July 20
"The hardest arithmetic to master is that which enables us to count our blessings."
–Eric Hoffer

July 21

"To live a life of gratitude is to open our eyes to the countless ways in which we are supported by the world around us."
–Gregg Krech

July 22

"Gratitude and love are always multiplied when you give them freely. They are an infinite source of contentment and prosperous energy." –Jim Fargiano

July 23

"The best way to show gratitude to God is to accept everything, even my problems, with joy." –Mother Teresa

July 24

"God has two dwellings: one in heaven and the other in a meek and thankful heart."

~Izaak Walton

July 25

"Gratitude should not be just a reaction to getting what you want, but an all-the-time gratitude, the kind where you notice the little things and where you constantly look for good, even in unpleasant situations. Start bringing gratitude to your experiences, instead of waiting for a positive experience in order to feel grateful." ~Marelisa Fábrega

July 26

"The LORD is my light and my salvation; whom shall I fear? The LORD is the strength of my life; of whom shall I be afraid?" –Psalm 27:1 (NKJV)

July 27

"[Gratitude] turns what we have into enough, and more. It turns denial into acceptance, chaos into order, confusion into clarity...it makes sense of our past, brings peace for today and creates a vision for tomorrow." –Melody Beattie

July 28

"He who does not reflect his life back to God in gratitude does not know himself." –Albert Schweitzer

June 29

"God is not less powerful because He allows us to endure hardship and pain. Be grateful for His divine wisdom. God knows exactly what He is doing even if it doesn't make sense to us. When we trust Him, we will discover He deeply loves us. God will always sustain us no matter what the outcome of our experiences might be."
~C. Chérie Hardy

July 30

"Feeling grateful or appreciative of someone or something in your life actually attracts more of the things that you appreciate and value in your life."
~Christiane Northrup

July 31

"Be grateful for the only living and true God who has good plans for us. He wants to give us peace and not evil. He delights in giving us a future and a hope. He not only listens to us, but answers our prayers. Our magnificent God promises to be available as we seek Him out." ~C. Chérie Hardy (Based on Jeremiah 29:11-12)

August 1

"I try hard to hold fast to the truth that a full and thankful heart cannot entertain great conceits. When brimming with gratitude, one's heartbeat must sure result in outgoing love, the finest emotion we can ever know."
~William Griffith Wilson

August 2

"Praise the Lord, my soul; and forget not all his benefits..." –Psalm 103:2 (NIV)

August 3

"Who can you call at three o'clock in the morning? Many people, even our relatives won't pick up the phone. However, God is available every day and all day. He is willing to listen and talk to us all 1,440 minutes of each day. No can do this for us, and perhaps that is exactly how God wants it. He must be our main meal and everyone else is like dessert, something extra. Be grateful for a God who is never too busy, too tired or too frustrated to fellowship with us!" –C. Chérie Hardy

August 4

"Perhaps it takes a purer faith to praise God for unrealized blessings than for those we once enjoyed or those we enjoy now."
~A. W. Tozer

August 5

"On the recollection of so many and great favors and blessings, I now, with a high sense of gratitude, presume to offer up my sincere thanks to the Almighty, the Creator and Preserver." ~William Bartram

August 6

"Choosing to be positive and having a grateful attitude is going to determine how you're going to live your life." ~Joel Osteen

August 7

"God didn't make just one kind of flower. He created roses, daisies, pansies, tulips, gardenias... He made many kinds of humans, too. No human being shares the same fingerprint as another. This is the way God intended things to be. Express gratitude for your uniqueness. You can stop trying to be a clone of someone else when you know God wanted no one to be *exactly* like you!"
–C. Chérie Hardy

August 8

"When you are grateful, fear disappears and abundance appears."
–Anthony Robbins

August 9

"Life without thankfulness is devoid of love and passion. Hope without thankfulness is lacking in fine perception. Faith without thankfulness lacks strength and fortitude. Every virtue divorced from thankfulness is maimed and limps along the spiritual road."
—John Henry Jowett

August 10

"Whatever happens in your life, no matter how troubling things might seem, do not enter the neighborhood of despair. Even when all the doors remain closed, God will open up a new path only for you! Be thankful!" —Elif Shafak

August 11

"I shall not die, but live, and declare the works of the LORD. The LORD has chastened me severely, but He has not given me over to death."
–Psalm 118:17-18 (NKJV)

August 12

"Every day I've got to be thankful that I am alive, and you never know—the cliché is, I guess, you could get hit by a bus tomorrow, so you'd better be at peace with whatever you got going at the moment."
–Joseph Gordon-Levitt

August 13

"Whenever people choose to excommunicate us from their lives, there is always pain. Whenever human bonds are broken, there is season of discomfort as we adjust to the loss of the familiar. However, remember this fact as you work to make peace about the situation: if you lived without the person before, you will not die due to the person's departure from your life. Be grateful that you don't have to stop living when someone decides to say, 'good bye'." –C. Chérie Hardy

August 14

"If you can't be thankful for what you receive, be thankful for what you escape." –Author Unknown

August 15

"If you hold up your head with a smile on your face and are truly thankful, you are blessed because the majority can, but most do not." –Author Unknown

August 16

"Keep your eyes open to your mercies. The man who forgets to be thankful has fallen asleep in life."
–Robert Louis Stevenson

August 17

"Forget about what you have lost; be thankful for what you still have; look ahead to what is yet to come." –Author Unknown

August 18

"The LORD is gracious and full of compassion, slow to anger and great in mercy. The LORD is good to all, and His tender mercies are over all His works."
–Psalm 145:8-9 (NKJV)

August 19

"I will praise You, O LORD, with my whole heart; I will tell of all Your marvelous works. I will be glad and rejoice in You; I will sing praises to Your name, O Most High."
–Psalm 9:1-2 (NKJV)

August 20

"See how many are better off than you are, but consider how many are worse."
–Seneca, the Elder

August 21

"Be grateful for good men in the world. God has blessed all of us to know men who are selfless, humble, and loving. These men not only love their wives and children, but sacrifice their time and resources to help others in need." ~C. Chérie Hardy

August 22

"Gratitude doesn't change the scenery. It merely washes clean the glass you look through so you can clearly see the colors." ~Richelle E. Goodrich

August 23

"Who does not thank for little will not thank for much." ~Estonian Proverb

August 24

"Gratitude can transform common days into thanksgivings, turn routine jobs into joy, and change ordinary opportunities into blessings." –William Arthur Ward

August 25

"Gratitude is a form of worship in its own right, as it implies the acceptance and power greater than yourself." –Stephen Richards

August 26

"Gratitude is when memory is stored in the heart and not in the mind."
–Lionel Hampton

August 27

"The LORD opens the eyes of the blind; the LORD raises those who are bowed down; the LORD loves the righteous. The LORD watches over the strangers; He relieves the fatherless and widow; but the way of the wicked He turns upside down."
–Psalm 146:8-9 (NKJV)

August 28

"I woke up this morning with devout thanksgiving for my friends, the old and the new." –Ralph Waldo Emerson

August 29

"Give thanks to unknown blessings already on their way." –Author Unknown

August 30

"At the heart of all frustration is desire. It is when people become obsessed with something they want and do not have. There are only two ways to solve this problem: (1) set out to get what you want if you think you can, and (2) make peace about not having what you want. In other words, decide to be content and grateful even if you never get the object of your desire. If you have lived without it before, you can keep living without it now."
–C. Chérie Hardy

August 31

"Gratitude is the single most important ingredient of living a successful and fulfilled life." –Jack Canfield

94

September 1

"God is always trying to teach us something. There is a lesson in every experience we have; we can gain great wisdom from both the pleasant and uncomfortable moments in our lives. Be grateful that our loving God is a master teacher who will never give you a failing grade. Focus, humble yourself, and come to His tutorial. He is diligent and caring, and most importantly, desires that you succeed on all of life's tests." ~C. Chérie Hardy

September 2

"When you appreciate what you have, what you have appreciates in value." ~Author Unknown

September 3

"We need to thank all of our troops, and particularly those for whom we can never express enough gratitude for they have given their lives so that all of us may be free and our democracy can be a shining for the rest of the world." –Virgil Goode

September 4

"I know how to be brought low, and I know how to abound. In any and every circumstance, I have learned the secret of facing plenty and hunger, abundance and need. I can do all things through [Christ] who strengthens me."
–Philippians 4:12-13 (ESV)

September 5

"God has given us the gift of fear to let us know what is dangerous so that we will stay away from it. It's an emotion that all humans have. The key is not to let the wrong kind of fear take control of your life. This fear is paralyzing and stops us from pursuing God's plans for us. Thank God for the right kind of fear and be grateful for the wisdom to distinguish one kind from the other." –C. Chérie Hardy

September 6

"Those who have the ability to be grateful are the ones who have the ability to achieve greatness." –Steve Maraboli

September 7

"When something happens to you and you don't understand it, learn to thank God anyway. Pray that God's truth will be revealed to you. Ask Him for clarity, direction, and understanding."
−C. Chérie Hardy

September 8

"In our deepest night of trouble and sorrow God gives us so much to be thankful for so that we need never cease our singing. With all our wisdom and foresight we can take a lesson in gladness and gratitude from the happy bird that sings all night, as if the day were not long enough to tell its joy."
−Samuel Taylor Coleridge

September 9

"The LORD is righteous in all His ways. Gracious in all His works. The LORD is near to all who call upon Him, to all who call upon Him in truth. He will fulfill the desire of those who fear Him; He also will hear their cry and save them. The LORD preserves all who love Him, but all the wicked He will destroy."
–Psalm 145:17-20 (NKJV)

September 10

"I may not be where I want to be but I'm thankful for not being where I used to be."
— Habeeb Akande

September 11

"Without darkness, we may never know how bright the starts shine. Without battles, we could not know what victory feels like. Without adversity, we may never appreciate the abundance in our lives. Be thankful, not only for the easy times, but for every experience that has made you who you are."
–Julie-Anne

September 12

"Gratefulness is the key to a happy life that we hold in our hands, because if we are not grateful, then no matter how much we have, we will not be happy—because we will always want to have something else or something more."—David Steindl-Rast

September 13

"Be grateful for the courageous men and women who tirelessly risk their lives on a daily basis to serve, save, and protect all people from danger." ~C. Chérie Hardy

September 14

"A thankful person is thankful under all circumstances. A complaining soul complains even if he lives in paradise."
~Baha'u'llah

September 15

"If God doesn't take us out of the fire, let us thank Him for making us fireproof."
~C. Chérie Hardy

September 16

"When [children] give you a gift, even if it is a rock they just picked up, exude gratitude. It might be the only thing they have to give and they have chosen to give it to you."
–Dean Jackson

September 17

"Go outside and look at the clouds. Be grateful for what you see because it is evidence that there is something greater than mankind in charge of the universe. If men can't make a car that won't break down, you know they didn't make the stars, moon, and sun. God made you, too; He considers you a priceless masterpiece in His art collection." –C. Chérie Hardy

September 18

"In our daily lives, we must see that it is not happiness that makes us grateful, but gratefulness that makes us happy."
–Albert Clarke

September 19

"If gratitude is due from children to their earthly parents, how much more is the gratitude of the great family of men due to our Father in heaven?" –Hosea Ballou

September 20

"The moment one gives close attention to anything, even a blade of grass it becomes a mysterious, awesome, indescribably magnificent world in itself." –Henry Miller

September 21

"On this day a few years ago, my life was changed due to a flood. When the waters had receded and I returned to my home, the first thing I was saw was amazing. On the dining room table was a photo album of my daughter. Miraculously, it had sustained very little water damage. God was saying to me, 'If Felicia had been here...' That day, I had lost most of the material things I owned, but God had spared our lives. I am grateful for His mercy." –C. Chérie Hardy

September 22

"You gotta look for the good in the bad, the happy in your sad, the gain in your pain, and what makes you grateful and not hateful."—Karen Salmansohn

September 23
"When someone saves your life and gives you life, there's gratitude and humility; there's a time you've been so blessed you realize you've been given another chance at life that maybe you didn't deserve."
–Pat Summerall

September 24
"Gratitude is the fairest blossom which springs from the soul; and the heart of man knoweth none more fragrant."
–Hosea Ballou

September 25
"Gratitude consists of being more aware of what you have, than what you don't."
–Author Unknown

September 26

"Do not indulge in dreams of having what you have not, but reckon up the chief of the blessings you do possess, and then thankfully remember how you would crave for them if they were not yours."
–Marcus Aurelius

September 27

"One looks back with appreciation to the brilliant teachers, but with gratitude to those who touched our human feelings. The curriculum is so much necessary raw material, but warmth is the vital element for the growing plant and for the soul of the child." –Carl Jung

September 28
"The LORD is my shepherd; I shall not want." –Psalm 23:1 (NKJV)

September 29
"What well-bred woman would refuse her heart to a man who had just saved her life? Not one; and gratitude is a short cut which speedily leads to love."
–Théophile Gautier

September 30
"The ungrateful heart discovers no mercies; but the thankful heart will find, in every hour, some heavenly blessings."
–Henry Ward Beecher

October 1

"Because you can laugh in your heart or laugh aloud, give God thanks. You can laugh for free, 24 hours a day and seven days a week if you wanted to. Make sure you laugh today and let God know how grateful you are for this awesome and healing gift." ~C. Chérie Hardy

October 2

"Thanksgiving comes to us out of prehistoric dimness, universal to all ages and all faiths. At whatever straws we must grasp, there is always a time for gratitude and new beginnings." ~J. Robert Moskin

October 3

"You cannot be grateful and be bitter. You cannot be grateful and unhappy. You cannot be grateful and without hope. You cannot be grateful and unloving. So just be grateful." ~Author Unknown

October 4

"It might be hard, but learn how to express gratitude for rejection. In the end, you will discover that God determined it was for your protection." ~C. Chérie Hardy

October 5

"Be grateful for whomever comes, because each has been sent as a guide from beyond." ~Jalal ad-Din Rumi

October 6

"When our perils are past, shall our gratitude sleep? No! Here's to the Pilot that weathered the storm."
~George Canning

October 7

"Blessed are those who are persecuted for righteousness' sake, for theirs is the kingdom of heaven."
~Matthew 5:10 (NKJV)

October 8

"If people offer their help or wisdom as you go through life, accept it gratefully. You can learn much from those who have gone before you." ~Edmund O'Neill

October 9

"When my father and my mother forsake me,
then the LORD will take care of me."
–Psalm 27:10 (NKJV)

October 10

"Be thankful that God looks at the heart
of a person and not his outer appearance."
–C. Chérie Hardy

October 11

"For there is nothing hidden which will not
be revealed nor has anything been kept
secret but that it should come to light."
–Matthew 4:22 (NKJV)

October 12

"Though they only take a second to say, thank-you's leave a warm feeling behind that can last for hours." –Kent Allan Rees

October 13

"Our first order of business is to stay positive; to entertain only positive possibilities; to imagine only affirmative alternatives; to surround ourselves with wholly uplifting, life-affirming people and influences; to align ourselves solely with the greater good so that our actions will be born of only the finest of our best intentions." –Donna Henes

October 14

"Live your life so that the fear of death can never enter your heart. When you arise in the morning, give thanks for the morning light. Give thanks for your life and strength. Give thanks for your food and for the joy of living. And if perchance you see no reason for giving thanks, rest assured the fault is in yourself." ~Chief Tecumseh

October 15

"It is good to be grateful for our creativity which whenever we share it becomes a timeless blessing." ~C. Chérie Hardy

October 16

"Keep your face to the sunshine and you cannot see the shadows." ~Helen Keller

113

October 17
"When you realize that there is nothing lacking, the whole world belongs to you."
–Lao Tzu

October 18
"Even though we can't have all we want, we ought to be thankful we don't get all of what we deserve." –Author Unknown

October 19
"Gratitude is the sign of noble souls."
–Aesop

October 20
"Gratitude is a fruit of great cultivation; you do not find it among gross people."
–Samuel Johnson

October 21

"I have learned that in every circumstance that comes my way, I can choose to respond in one of two ways: I can whine or I can worship! And I can't worship without giving thanks. It just isn't possible. When we choose the pathway of worship and giving thanks, especially in the midst of difficult circumstances, there is a fragrance, a radiance that issues forth out of our lives to bless the Lord and others."
–Nancy Leigh DeMoss

October 22

"Gratitude is the moral memory of mankind."
–Georg Simmel

October 23

"Blessed are those who mourn, for they shall be comforted."
–Matthew 5:4 (NKJV)

October 24

"Two men look out from the same prison window; one sees bars and the other sees the stars." –Frederick Langbridge

October 25

"Gratitude is one of the sweet shortcuts to finding peace of mind and happiness inside. No matter what is going on outside of us, there's always something we could be grateful for." –Barry Neal Kaufman

October 26

"Have you ever been in a bad situation? Did you ever get out of it? The answer is probably 'yes' to both questions. If God helped you in the past, He will surely aid you in the future. Let God's work history remind you that everything is going to be alright! Be grateful for the memories of His redemptive and restorative power."

–C. Chérie Hardy

October 27

"Blessed is everyone who fears the LORD, who walks in His ways."

–Psalm 128:1 (NKJV)

October 28

"Every once and awhile God allows you to stub your toe. This is a kind of reminder to be grateful for the miraculous body attached to it." –Richelle E. Goodrich

October 29

"If you suffer, thank God! It is a sure sign that you are alive." –Elbert Hubbard

October 30

"Gratitude is the energy of faith."
–Author Unknown

October 31

"Enough is a feast." –Buddhist Proverb

November 1

"It is chiefly through books that we enjoy communion with superior minds...In the best books, authors talk to us, give us their most precious thoughts and pour their souls into ours. God be thanked for books."
–William Ellery Channing

November 2

"The secret of happiness is to count your blessings while others are adding up their troubles." –William Penn

November 3

"Not what we say about our blessings, but how we use them, is the true measure of our thanksgiving." –W. T. Purkiser

November 4

"All the great questions must be raised by great voices, and the greatest voice is the voice of the people—speaking out in prose, or painting or poetry or music; speaking out—in homes and halls, streets and farms, courts and cafes—let that voice speak and the stillness you hear will be the gratitude of mankind." –Robert F. Kennedy

November 5

"I will praise You with my whole heart; before the gods I will sing praises to You. I will worship toward Your holy temple, and praise Your name for Your lovingkindness and Your truth..."
–Psalm 138:1-2a (NKJV)

November 6

"No longer forward nor behind, I look in hope or fear; but grateful take the good I find, the best of now and here."
~John Greenleaf Whittier

November 7

"Look at everything as though you were seeing it either for the first time or last time. Then your time on earth will be filled with [gratitude]." ~Betty Smith

November 8

"Blessed are the pure in heart, for they shall see God." ~Matthew 5:8 (NKJV)

November 9
"Every day may not be good but there is good in every day." ~Author Unknown

November 10
"Don't just thank God for the light; thank Him also for darkness. We have more appreciation for our times of peace when we have endured great chaos and turmoil."
~C. Chérie Hardy

November 11
"No duty is more urgent than that of returning thanks." ~Saint Ambrose

November 12

"While email is probably faster, take a few moments to write an old-fashioned thank-you letter. Express your gratitude to the people who have inspired and supported you. Your success is partly due to their help. They will appreciate getting your beautiful letter instead of a bill."
–C. Chérie Hardy

November 13

"Remember the good times and be strong during the difficult ones. Love always, smile often and thank God for every moment!"
–Ritu Ghatourey

November 14
"Be grateful that God made crooked paths straight for you and protected you from the snakes behind the rocks."
–C. Chérie Hardy

November 15
"When you practice gratefulness, there is a sense of respect towards others."
—The Dalai Lama

November 16
"Gratitude becomes spiritual, a spiritual virtue and a spiritual emotion, when we are moved in our response by a God-centered view of the three: gift, recipient, and giver."
–Ray A.

November 17

"Be grateful for our loving, compassionate, and omnipotent God—not just because of what He can give us, but whom He can help us become."
~C. Chérie Hardy

November 18

"Difficulties are opportunities to better things; they are stepping stones to greater experiences. Perhaps someday you will be thankful for some temporary failure in a particular direction. When one door closes, another always opens." ~Author Unknown

November 19

"The essence of all beautiful art, all great art, is gratitude." ~Friedrich Nietzche

November 20
"Love in action is the best way to show how grateful you are for your blessings."
~C. Chérie Hardy

November 21
"An attitude of gratitude brings great things." ~Yogi Bhajan

November 22
"To bring gratitude into your life, you can deliberately meditate on all the things in your own life that help you or give you pleasure." ~Melanie Greenberg

November 23
"An attitude of gratitude brings opportunities." ~Author Unknown

November 24

"Nothing has turned out as we expected! It never does. Life's under no obligation to give us what we expect. We take what we get and are thankful it's no worse than it is."
–Author Unknown

November 25

"Happiness is not based on the level of your possessions in life; rather it is based on your perceptions of life and its circumstances. Never permit circumstances to steal your gratitude about your life."
–Edmond Mbiaka

November 26

"If you have lived, take thankfully the past."
–John Dryden

November 27
"When life gives you a hundred reasons to cry, show life that you have a thousand reasons to smile." –Author Unknown

November 28
"Be thankful for each new challenge because it will build your strength and character."–Author Unknown

November 29
"Each day I am thankful for: nights that turned into morning, friends that turned into family, dreams that turned into reality and likes that turned into love."
–Ritu Ghatourey

November 30

"Where can I go from Your Spirit? Or where can I flee from Your presence? If I ascend into heaven, You are there; if I make my bed in hell, behold, You are there, if I take the wings of the morning, and dwell in the uttermost parts of the sea, even there Your hand shall lead me."
–Psalm 139:7-9 (NKJV)

December 1

"It is not good for all our wishes to be filled; through sickness we recognize the value of health; through evil, the value of good; through hunger, the value of food; through exertion, the value of rest." ~Greek Proverb

December 2
"I had the blues because I had no shoes until upon the street I met a man who had no feet." –Author Unknown

December 3
"Take a moment to thank God for your life. If you were not special, you would have never been born." –C. Chérie Hardy

December 4
"Don't count your loss but instead cherish what you [still] have and plan what you want to gain, for the past never returns, but the future may fulfill the loss." –Nishan Panwar

December 5
"Whatever our individual troubles and challenges may be, it's important to pause every now and then to appreciate all that we have, on every level." –Shakti Gawain

December 6
"Blessed are the merciful, for they shall obtain mercy." –Matthew 5:7 (NKJV)

December 7
"Gratitude can lead to feelings of love, appreciation, generosity, and compassion, which further opens our hearts and helps rewire our brains to fire in more positive ways." –Melanie Greenberg

December 8
"Let us serve the world soulfully. The pay
we will receive for our service will be in the
currency of gratitude—God's gratitude."
—Sri Chinmoy

December 9
"The most fortunate are those who have a
wonderful capacity to appreciate again and
again, freshly and naively, the basic goods
of life, with awe, pleasure, wonder, and even
ecstasy." —Abraham Maslov

December 10
"If a fellow isn't thankful for what he's got,
he isn't likely to be thankful for what he's
going to get." —Frank A. Clark

December 11

"Be grateful for wisdom which is more valuable than any tangible thing you own. God's wisdom gives us clarity, guidance, and truth. It sustains us through murky waters." ~C. Chérie Hardy

December 12

"Learn to get in touch with silence within yourself, and know that everything in this life has a purpose. There are no mistakes, no coincidences, all events are blessings given to us to learn from."
— Elizabeth Kubler-Ross

December 13

"Wise men count their blessings; fools their problems." ~Author Unknown

December 14

"I may not be popular, but I have nice friends. I may not be rich, but I have what I need. I may not be liked by many, but I am loved by those who matter most."
–Tori Vazquez

December 15

"A grateful mindset can set you free from the prison of disempowerment and the shackles of misery." –Steve Maraboli

December 16

"Appreciation can make a day, even change a life. Your willingness to put it into words is all that is necessary." –Margaret Cousins

December 17

"I am thankful, that sometimes I am the black sky for your stars to shine against. I am the desert where your oasis lives. I am the thorn where your rose blossoms. I am the oyster where your pearl forms. I am the mine where your diamond will shape." –Avantika

December 18

"Whatever you appreciate and give thanks for will increase in your life."
–Sanaya Roman

December 19

"Be grateful for God's spiritual mirror that allows us to see ourselves as we really are."
–C. Chérie Hardy

December 20

"It is necessary, then, to cultivate the habit of being grateful for every good thing that comes to you, and to give thanks continuously. And because all things have contributed to your advancement, you should include all things in your gratitude."
–Wallace Watties

December 21

One of the very first things I figured out about this life... is that it's better to be a grateful personal than a grumpy one because you have to live in the same world either way, and if you are grateful, you have more fun." –Barbara Kingsolver

December 22

"No one is capable of gratitude as one who has emerged from the kingdom of night."
~Elie Wiesel

December 23

"No gesture is too small when done with gratitude." ~Oprah Winfrey

December 24

"God's greatest gift to us is love. Love doesn't from people, it comes *through* them. God's unconditional love makes our lives richer, stronger, and more purposeful. No matter how busy your life might be, take a moment everyday to express gratitude for God's amazing love." ~C. Chérie Hardy

December 25

"The exact date and time of Jesus' birth is less important to me than knowing that he *was* born. Whether a person views Jesus as a historical figure, spiritual savior or both, no one can deny that he was the most awesome human being to ever walk the planet. A record of Jesus' amazing life, legacy, and teachings can be found in the Holy Bible. My gratitude for this knowledge is indescribable. Nothing or no one has been a greater source of comfort and guidance for me. Jesus' teachings will remain timeless and have limitless power to all mankind. They are true because they are self-evident to each soul that follows them."

–C. Chérie Hardy

December 26

"Let everything that has breath praise the LORD." –Psalm 150:6 (NKJV)

December 27

"When we eat fruit, we should think of the person who planted the tree." –Vietnamese Proverb

December 28

"We should be grateful for the people in our lives who won't allow us to complain. It's a blessing to know people who lovingly help us see the silver lining behind every dark cloud." –C. Chérie Hardy

December 29

"Gratitude goes beyond the 'mine' and 'thine' and claims the truth that all of life is a pure gift. In the past I always thought of gratitude as a spontaneous response to the awareness of gifts received, but I now I realize that gratitude can be lived as a discipline. The discipline of gratitude is the explicit effort to acknowledge that all I am and have is given to me as a gift of love, a gift to be celebrated with joy."
~Henri J.M. Nouwen

December 30

"Gratitude begins when [our] sense of entitlement ends." ~Author Unknown

December 31

"Let us rise up and be thankful, for if we didn't learn a lot today, at least we learned a little, and if we didn't learn a little, at least we didn't get sick, and if we got sick, at least we didn't die; so, let us all be thankful."

~ Siddhartha Gautama

Other books by C. Chérie Hardy

Daily Pearls: Wisdom and Inspiration for Each Day of the Year

Love Doesn't Hurt: Life Lessons for Women

Wise and Wonderful: Life Lessons for Single Mothers

Encouragement for the Grieving Heart: 365 Inspirational Quotes and Scriptures for Coping with Loss

Guess What I Can See with My Microscope!

This Beautiful Hair of Mine (children's book)

Three Nights in December (novel)

The Orange Zebra (children's book)

Teach. Learn. Inspire.
A 180-Day Inspirational Journal for Teachers

Morning Chai with God: Inspirational Messages that Strengthen Your Faith

Let's stay connected!

Website: www.avantgardebooks.net

Facebook: @avantgardebooks100

Twitter: @Avant_GardeBks

Instagram: @avantgardebooks

Email: avantgardebooks@gmail.com

www.ingramcontent.com/pod-product-compliance
Lightning Source LLC
Chambersburg PA
CBHW060015050426
42448CB00012B/2766